Technology That Every CIO Needs To Know About

How CIOs Can Stay On Top Of the Changes in the Technology That Powers the Company

"Practical, proven techniques that will show you how to use technology to make your company more successful"

Dr. Jim Anderson

Published by:
Blue Elephant Consulting
Tampa, Florida

Copyright © 2014 by Dr. Jim Anderson

All rights reserved. No part of this book may be reproduced of transmitted in any form or by any means, electronic or mechanical, including photocopying, recording or by any information storage and retrieval system without written permission of the publisher, except for inclusion of brief quotations in a review.

Printed in the United States of America

Library of Congress Control Number: 2014918151

ISBN-13: 978-1502760746
ISBN-10: 1502760746

Warning – Disclaimer

The purpose of this book is to educate and entertain. This book does not promise or guarantee that anyone following the ideas, tips, suggestions, techniques or strategies will be successful. The author, publisher and distributor(s) shall have neither liability nor responsibility to anyone with respect to any loss or damage caused, or alleged to be caused, directly or indirectly by the information contained in this book.

Recent Books By The Author

Product Management

- How Product Managers Can Grow Their Career: How Product Managers Can Find And Succeed In The Right Job

- Product Management Secrets: Techniques For Product Managers To Boost Product Sales And Increase Customer Satisfaction

Public Speaking

- Plan For Success: How To Plan Your Next Speech: How to plan a speech in order to achieve your goals and delight your audience

- How To Become A Better Speaker By Changing How You Speak: Change techniques that will transform a speech into a memorable event

CIO Skills

- What CIOs Need To Know About Working With Partners: Techniques For CIOs To Use In Order To Be Able To Successfully Work With Partners

- How CIOs Can Make Innovation Happen: Tips And Techniques For CIOs To Use In Order To Make Innovation Happen In Their IT Department

IT Manager Skills

- How IT Managers Can Make Innovation Happen: Tips And Techniques For IT Managers To Use In Order To Make Innovation Happen In Their Teams

- Secrets Of Effective Leadership For IT Managers: Tips And Techniques That IT Managers Can Use In Order To Develop Leadership Skills

Negotiating

- Learn How To Signal In Your Next Negotiation: How To Develop The Skill Of Effective Signaling In A Negotiation In Order To Get The Best Possible Outcome

- Learn The Skill Of Exploring In A Negotiation: How To Develop The Skill Of Exploring What Is Possible In A Negotiation In Order To Reach The Best Possible Deal

Miscellaneous

- The Internet-Enabled Successful School District Superintendent: How To Use The Internet To Boost Parental Involvement In Your Schools

- Power Distribution Unit (PDU) Secrets: What Everyone Who Works In A Data Center Needs To Know!

Note: See a complete list of books by Dr. Jim Anderson at the back of this book.

Acknowledgements

Any book like this one is the result of years of real-world work experience. In my over 25 years of working for 7 different firms, I have met countless fantastic people and I've been mentored by some truly exceptional ones. Although I've probably forgotten some of the people who made me the person that I am today, here is my attempt to finally give them the recognition that they so truly deserve:

- Thomas P. Anderson
- Art Puett
- Bobbi Marshall
- Bob Boggs

Dr. Jim Anderson

This book is dedicated to my family: Lori, Maddie, Nick, and Ben. None of this would have been possible without their constant love and support.

Thanks for always believing in me and providing me with the strength to always be willing to go out there and be my best for you.

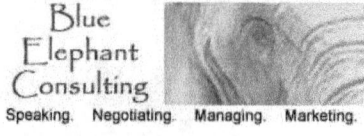

Table Of Contents

TECHNOLOGY THAT EVERY CIO NEEDS TO KNOW ABOUT 8

ABOUT THE AUTHOR 10

CHAPTER 1: WHY NOSQL IS THE WRONG CHOICE FOR A CIO — SOMETIMES 15

CHAPTER 2: CIO LESSONS FROM THE ROLLOUT OF THE U.S. HEALTHCARE SOFTWARE 20

CHAPTER 3: CIOS AND THE PROBLEM WITH FOOD STAMPS 25

CHAPTER 4: THE 7 STAGES OF BIG DATA ANALYTICS THAT EVERY CIO NEEDS TO KNOW ABOUT 30

CHAPTER 5: CIOS NEED TO BE ON THE LOOKOUT FOR PROPRIETARY SOLUTIONS DISGUISED AS STANDARDS 34

CHAPTER 6: CIOS NEED TO PLAN FOR THE END OF A CLOUD RELATIONSHIP 38

CHAPTER 7: BIG DATA MEANS 5 BIG PROBLEMS FOR CIOS 42

CHAPTER 8: QUESTIONS ABOUT THE CLOUD THAT EVERY CIO SHOULD BE ASKING 46

CHAPTER 9: WHY CIOS NEED TO GET GOOD AT REUSING TECHNOLOGY 51

CHAPTER 10: WHEN IT COMES TO DATA MINING – IS THE CIO IN CHARGE? 55

CHAPTER 11: THE PROBLEM WITH GLITCHES 59

CHAPTER 12: PERHAPS THE IT HELP DESK IS NO LONGER NEEDED? .. 63

Technology That Every CIO Needs To Know About

As the CIO of your company, it's your job to stay on top of all of the different forms of technology that the company uses to accomplish its business goals. This task is made even harder by all of the changes that are always occurring in the various technology fields.

As the CIO you need to understand how to pick the correct type of database to be used on projects. You need to watch the rollout of other large-scale IT projects and learn from them: what went right and what went wrong.

The IT world that we live in these days seems to be awash in big data. As the CIO you are going to be called on to make important decisions about how your firm handles its own big data issues. You'll need to pick the right solutions and ensure that you are not being locked into proprietary vendor solutions.

It seems as though every firm is in the process of moving more and more of their computing into "the cloud". As the CIO it's going to be your responsibility to make sure that you have a plan for how you want to handle your cloud vendor at the start of the relationship as well as at the end of it.

The value of the IT department to the rest of the company becomes apparent when other departments need your help in sifting through vast quantities of data. Make sure that you have a plan for how you are going to do this. Also make sure that you have a help desk that is going to be ready to provide your customers with the support that they'll need.

This book has been written in order to provide you with a great starting point for ensuring that you've done everything that you can to stay on top of the latest technology that is being used by your company. Follow the suggestions in this book and you'll know what technologies to use and when to use them.

For more information on what it takes to be a great CIO, check out my blog, The Accidental Successful CIO, at:

www.TheAccidentalSuccessfulCIO.com

Good luck!

- Dr. Jim Anderson

About The Author

I must confess that I never set out to be a CIO. When I went to school, I studied Computer Science and thought that I'd get a nice job programming and that would be that. Well, at least part of that plan worked out!

My first job was working for Boeing on their F/A-18 fighter jet program. I spent my days programming fighter jet software in assembly language and I loved it. The U.S. government decided to save some money and went looking for other countries to sell this plane to. This put me into an unfamiliar role: I started to meet with foreign military officials and I ended up having to manage groups of engineers who were working on international projects.

Time moved on and so did I. I found myself working for Siemens, the big German telecommunications company. They were making phone switches and selling them to the seven U.S. phone companies. The problem was that the switches were too complicated. Customers couldn't tell the difference between one complicated phone switch from another complicated phone switch. Once again I found myself working with the sales and marketing teams to find ways to make the great technology that the engineers had developed understandable to both internal and external customers.

I've spent over 25 years working as an senior IT professional for both big companies and startups. This has given me an opportunity to learn what it takes to manage and IT department in ways that allow it to maximize its output while becoming a valuable part of the overall company.

I now live in Tampa Florida where I spend my time managing my consulting business, Blue Elephant Consulting, teaching college courses at the University of South Florida, and traveling to work with companies like yours to share the knowledge that I have about how to create and manage successful IT departments.

I'm always available to answer questions and I can be reached at:

Dr. Jim Anderson
Blue Elephant Consulting
Email: jim@BlueElephantConsulting.com
Facebook: http://goo.gl/1TVoK
Web: **www.BlueElephantConsulting.com**

"Unforgettable communication skills that will set your ideas free..."

Create IT Departments That Are Productive And A Valuable Asset To The Rest Of The Company !

Dr. Jim Anderson is available to provide training and coaching on the topics that are the most important to people who have to manage IT departments: how can I build a productive IT department (and keep it together) while at the same time providing the rest of the company with the IT services that they need?

Dr. Anderson believes that in order to both learn and remember what he says, speakers need to laugh. Each one of his speeches is full of fun and humor so that what he says "sticks" with everyone.

Dr. Anderson's CIO SkillsTraining Includes:

1. How to identify and attract the right type of IT workers to your IT department.
2. How to build relationships with the company's senior management in order to get the support that you need?
3. How to stay on top of changing technology and security issues so that you never get surprised?

Dr. Jim Anderson works with over 100 customers per year. To invite Dr. Anderson to work with you, contact him at:

Phone: 813-418-6970 or
Email: jim@BlueElephantConsulting.com

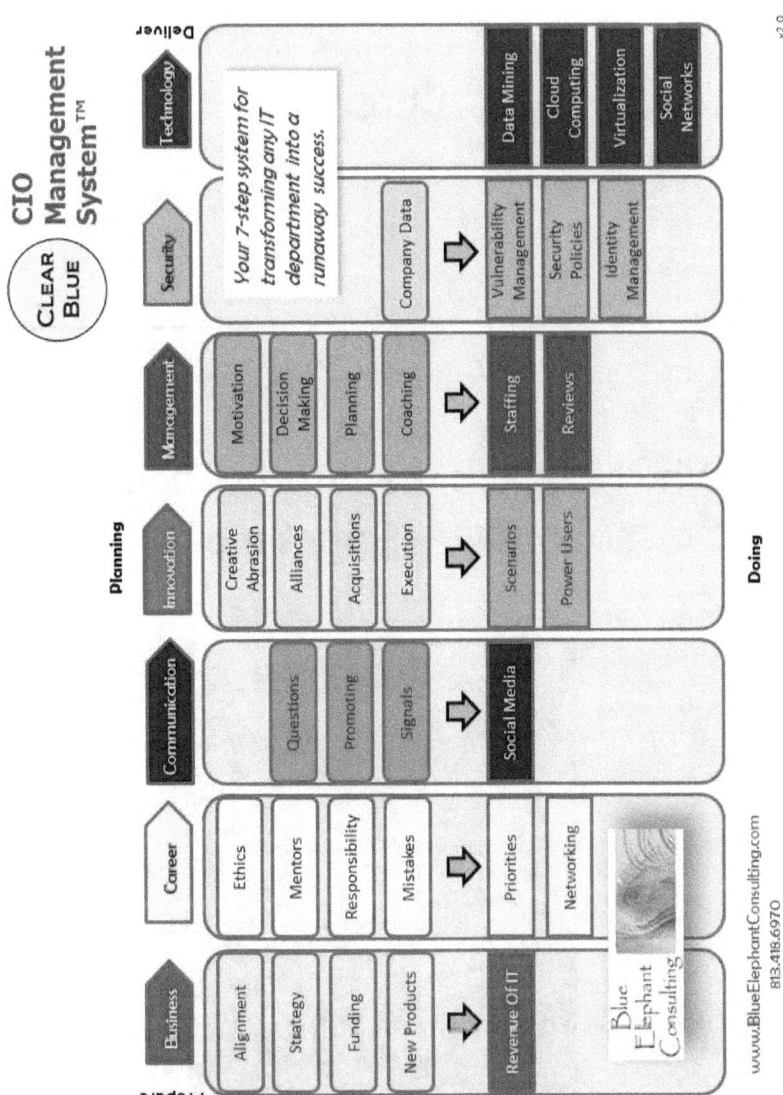

The **Clear Blue CIO Management System™** has been created to provide CIOs and senior IT managers with a clear roadmap for how to manage an IT department. This system shows CIOs what needs to be done and in what order to do it.

Chapter 1

Why NoSQL Is the Wrong Choice for A CIO – Sometimes

Chapter 1: Why NoSQL Is the Wrong Choice for A CIO — Sometimes

If you were to create a list of the buzz words that are filtering through the world of IT right now, **"NoSQL"** would have to be at the top of your list when you are talking about the importance of information technology. CIOs everywhere have decided that they've had enough of traditional databases and the high vendor fees that come with them. Open source noSQL databases appear to be the solution to all of their data processing needs. However, it turns out that this just isn't the case...

CIO's ACID Problem

When we get presented with a new technology, it can be all too easy to start to think that it is a solution that **we can apply to every problem that we are currently facing**. NoSQL is one such technology. However, the key is to realize that not all data that the IT department has been asked to process is created the same.

The data that the IT department has traditionally been asked to process **generally all looks similar**. This is the data that we feed to the company's mission critical systems. The acronym ACID has been created to describe this data:

- **Atomic:** each transaction is executed completely and can be rolled back if something goes wrong.

- **Consistent:** no transaction will be permitted to leave the database if for some reason it creates an inconsistency with the stored data.

- **Isolated:** each transaction does not affect another transactions

- **Durable:** before a transaction can be considered to be complete, it must first be recorded permanently in the database.

What CIOs Need To Know About BASE

In the new world of "big data" in which we find ourselves, clearly **not all data is going to meet the ACID criteria**. This is where the door of opportunity opens for noSQL databases.

When we start to consider web and social media applications, we start to have to deal with data that is **orders of magnitude** larger than most standard corporate databases. This means that developers need to become more flexible when dealing with this much information.

The data properties of this kind of new data workload have been captured in **the acronym BASE**. This stands for:

- **Basically Available:** just what it sounds like – the database is no longer required to be consistently real-time atomic.

- **Soft-State**: Database states are now permitted to change and expire instead of always having to be durable.

- **Eventual Consistency:** This flexibility is in contrast to a traditional ACID database's requirement to provide stringent transactional consistency.

Which Database Is The Right One To Use?

I'm sorry about this; however, although it's important to understand what kind of data set you are dealing with **(ACID or BASE)** , that's not going to be enough to tell you which type of SQL / noSQL database you need to use for your next IT project. The CIO's job is just a bit more complicated than that.

NoSQL will be the right database to use when you have BASE workloads that are clearly not ACID, **when you have a great deal of data**, and when you want to be able to run your database using commodity hardware and software.

There is one other point for you to consider when you are trying to decide between an SQL or noSQL solution. If you try to use an SQL database for an application that must deal with **high-volume workloads** that are delivered via the web, then you're going to see your database collapse because of the overhead. Instead, in these situations go with a noSQL solution.

What All of This Means for You

It's never been easy to be in the CIO position and lately it seems as though even those things that we thought that we had under control, like databases, are **undergoing significant changes**. One of these changes is the arrival of noSQL databases – when should we use them?

It turns out that **not all data sets are created equally**. Data that can be classified as being ACID are well suited to being processed by a standard database. However, data that can be classified as being BASE would be better handled by a noSQL database. Additional issues such as the quantity of data needs to be taken into consideration also.

What this means for you as a CIO is that what might have once been a fairly standard decision ("throw it into the database"), has now become yet another issue that you need to **take a careful look at** before making up your mind. Take the time to learn how to do this correctly and you'll find that you are making the right decisions for your company.

Chapter 2

CIO Lessons from the Rollout of the U.S. Healthcare Software

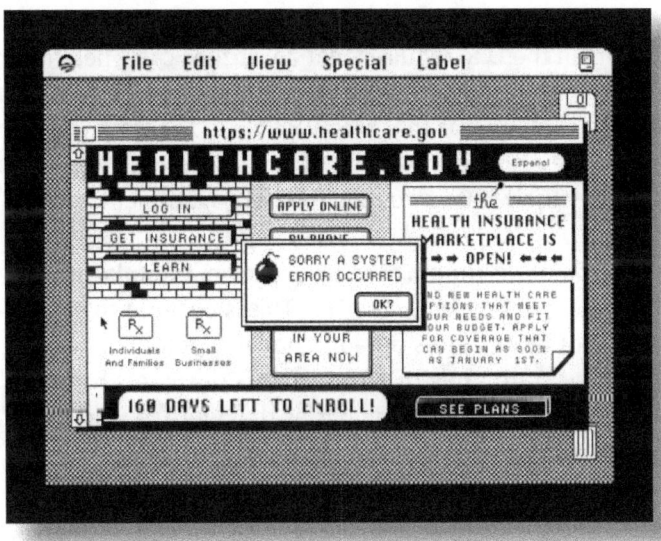

Chapter 2: CIO Lessons from the Rollout of the U.S. Healthcare Software

As CIOs we can always **be learning about the importance of information technology by watching what other IT organizations are doing**. A fantastic opportunity has recently shown up in the U.S. As part of the Obamacare overhaul of how healthcare is provided to U.S. citizens, a new web site was set up to allow every U.S. citizen an opportunity to register for healthcare insurance coverage. All has not gone well and that's where the real learning for CIOs is happening...

What Was Supposed To Happen

The Department of Health and Human Services is responsible for providing all Americans with the ability to sign up for the new health care system. The new health care law that has gone into effect in the U.S. requires that all citizens carry health care coverage. In order to get this coverage, they have to select from the health care options that are available in the state in which they live. They can do this **via an online web site** that is either provided by their state or by the federal government.

The government is **running the insurance marketplaces** in 36 of the 50 states that make up the U.S. This is because the governors of those states opted to not accept federal funding to expand their state's health care system. Consumers had until mid-December to sign up for policies that were to start on January 1st.

At their front end, the insurance marketplaces are essentially websites that consumers use to **compare health plans and enroll in coverage**. These websites link to data from other parts of the government, such as the Internal Revenue Service, and from health plans to verify eligibility and deliver subsidies for coverage. The Center for Consumer Information and Insurance

Oversight is one of the main offices within Medicare charged with developing the exchanges.

The healthcare exchanges are the cornerstone of the Affordable Care Act, President Obama's health insurance reform legislation enacted in March 2010. Since the passage of the law, government agencies, contractors and private insurers have been working on the design of the insurance exchanges. But implementation was only begun in earnest in the 12-18 months before its scheduled rollout. A Government Accountability Office report in June 2013 noted that, despite progress, "**much remains to be accomplished** within a relatively short amount of time."

What Really Happened and Why

When the rollout occurred, **there were glitches**. Some of the errors were simple things that should never have occurred like security question drop down boxes that were empty. However, there were other serious errors such as unavailable servers.

Ultimate responsibility for this very large scale IT system belongs to the Centers for Medicare & Medicaid Services. Tony Trenkle has the CIO job and is the Director of the Office of Information Services (OIS) in the Centers for Medicare and Medicaid Services (CMS). Ultimately, the proper operation of the online insurance marketplaces **is Tony's responsibility**.

Experts who have taken a close look at the federal web site and its supporting IT infrastructure have come away not being impressed. They report that there are both coding flaws and problems with the architecture of the system. One of the system's biggest flaws has to do with its ability to **verify the identity of a system user**. In order to do this it has to work correctly. Homeland Security has to send the citizenship information, IRS sends the income information, Social Security sends the Medicare eligibility information, and from the user's state it gets the Medicaid eligibility. Clearly there are a lot of API's and other interfaces at work here and it doesn't look like it was completely tested before being rolled out.

Experts who have examined the government web site are reporting that it appears to have been **built on a foundation of sloppy software.** Additionally, basic web application design techniques such as caching appear to not have been used. This coupled with web-traffic problems have resulted in the system being usable by only a small number of the roughly 9 million visitors that tried to use it the first day that it was in operation.

What All of This Means for You

The rollout of the IT systems that were required in order to support the Obamacare health initiative in the United States **turned into a bit of a mess on launch day.** The big question is why? The launch date had been known for a long time and you would think that the person in the CIO position would have had plenty of time to get all of the issues worked out.

The reasons that the rollout had such big problems were varied. Some of the problems can be traced to the simple fact that the system was **clearly not sized properly** – too many people tried to use it at the same time. This is a classic IT problem and should never have been an issue because we know how to deal with it. Another issue appears to have been the complexity associated with verifying users. This requires multiple systems to talk to each other on the back end and those interfaces appear to not be working correctly all the time.

Undoubtedly the IT issues with the new U.S. healthcare system will eventually be resolved. Having such a public facing system have issues almost insures that the right people will be working on it. However, if the CIO in charge had been doing his or her job, none of these **easily anticipated issues** would have occurred. As CIOs we need to take the time to learn from these mistakes and make sure that they never happen in our shop.

Chapter 3

CIOs and the Problem with Food Stamps

Chapter 3: CIOs and the Problem with Food Stamps

I'm hoping that you are not familiar with the U.S. food stamp program. It is a government funded program that provides people who are living below the poverty line with money that can only be spent on food. Clearly it's a critical program that demonstrates the importance of information technology and the people who are enrolled in it desperately need it. That's why it was unacceptable when the IT systems that support the program **stopped working**. Clearly the person who has the CIO job is the one to blame...

What Went Wrong With the Food Stamp System

The core of the problem is that the company Xerox is responsible for providing the back office IT systems that run the U.S. government's food stamp program. The Electronic Benefits Transfer (EBT) system allows recipients of government food stamps to purchase goods using a digital card with a set spending limit. A while ago, a power outage during a routine maintenance test **caused a temporary glitch in the food stamp program**.

One of the results of this glitch was that shoppers were able to sweep through the aisles at stores and buy as much as they could carry because **their preset spending limit had been removed**. This caused a great deal of concern at Walmart stores when shoppers started to show up at the checkout with fully loaded carts.

However, another side effect of the glitch was that other food stamp shoppers **were unable to purchase any food**. The glitch caused food stamp recipients in 17 states to lose access for much of a Saturday to the electronic system used by stores to verify their benefits. This left many unable to buy any groceries.

What Should Have Been Done

Clearly this situation should never have been allowed to happen. The Xerox team that designed the food stamp system **had not done the required amount of testing**. It appears as though they got themselves caught in the IT equivalent of a perfect storm: during a routine test of a backup system, a power glitch hit and that placed the system into a previously unknown state.

=====

Editor's Note: Many thanks to Carol Zierhoffer who wrote to me after this article was published in order to correct some misunderstandings on my part. I had stated that I felt that it was the Xerox CIO's fault that this outage had been allowed to happen. Carol pointed out that she was CIO at Xerox for just 18 months and had already left when the outage occurred (ouch — but that's for another article some other day).

Next she revealed that the CIO at Xerox does not have responsibility for the underlying applications that support the external offerings of the heritage ACS Company. Yes, yes there are all sorts of issues with this, but as Carol says, it's the way that things currently are.

In Carol's own words "By way of background, ACS was acquired by Xerox in Feb, 2010 and is now called Xerox Services (XS). XS has 100+ Strategic Business Units, each with their own IT organizations that are run independently by the Strategic Business Unit. That is how management chooses to run the company. The heritage Xerox side of the business is different, where the CIO does have full responsibility for all systems both customer facing and internal."

=====

The reason that I'm holding Xerox and their corporate CIO structure responsible for this is that we all know that events like this can happen. No, we can't predict exactly what they'll look like, but **we can almost certainly predict that they'll happen**. That's why it's the CIO's responsibility to make sure that the IT systems that they are responsible for have the ability to deal with unplanned circumstances.

There were two problems associated with this outage: the granting of unlimited spending to food stamp program participants and the inability of people to access the system. The removal of spending limits is a simple programming bug and effective code reviews would have detected this long ago. Much more unacceptable is **the extended outage** that a brief power outage caused. This is a fundamental system design problem that should never have occurred. Xerox needs to go back and fix things. Improving their code review procedures would be a good start, but redesigning the food stamp system to improve its reliability is a must.

What All of This Means for You

The U.S. food stamp program is a critical system that allows people to buy food who could not otherwise afford to do so. This means that it is **a mission critical system** and always has to be there to support these people who really can't speak for themselves. However, the system recently experienced an outage that prevented people from purchasing food for a period of time.

The outage is reported to have been caused by a routine test of the system's back up capabilities. As IT professionals, we can all understand how this type of testing can cause a ripple effect that could cause a system to shut down. However, when a system is a mission critical system, the design of the system has to take events like this into account and needs to have ways **to**

prevent it from impacting the vulnerable end users. Clearly this was not the case.

The person in the CIO position at Xerox has some answering to do. It's understood that the system may have been installed before she became CIO. However, as CIO it is her responsibility to **evaluate the level of risk associated with all of their systems** and clearly this has not been done for the food stamp application. Let us hope that she now realizes the importance of this system and that design changes will be made that will prevent an outage like this from ever happening again.

Chapter 4

The Seven Stages of Big Data Analytics That Every CIO Needs to Know About

Chapter 4: The 7 Stages of Big Data Analytics That Every CIO Needs to Know About

CIOs have always had to find ways to **deal with data**. Collecting it, storing it, processing it, and eventually archiving it. The arrival of the era of Big Data has almost overnight turned what was already a challenging task into a nearly impossible task. Everyone in the company understands the importance of information technology and they all believe that the IT department can solve all data related problems. Now what is a CIO supposed to do in order to understand what all of this data is trying to tell him or her?

The Seven Steps to Getting Value Out Of Your Big Data

All too often the person in the CIO job thinks that there is **some magical process** to deal with Big Data. They think that if they implement the right project, what will fall out of the other side is a set of analytical results that will be tailored for their business. Bad news – such a project does not exist.

Instead, what CIOs need to realize is that in order to get their hands around Big Data, they need to transition through **a series of 7 phases** in order to gradually show their IT department how to deal with the flood of data that is arriving at the doors of the IT department. Here are the 7 phases:

- **Surprise!:** This is the phase where the IT department starts to realize just exactly how much data is going to be coming their way. The implications of how they are going to both deal with and process this data are only now starting to be realized.

- **Data Vault:** In this phase the IT department swings into action. Processes and systems are set up to take the data and find ways to both store and secure it. Once that is done, with no further processing the raw data is then made available to the departments and groups who need it in order to do further processing on it.

- **Q&A:** In this phase, the IT department for the first time is able to process some of the data and start to answer questions about what happened in the past. This process is generally very manual and revolves around the creation of custom reports based on requests that come into the IT department.

- **Intelligence:** This phase is most easily recognized by the arrival of so-called "executive dashboards". However, what distinguishes it is that the reporting is now being automated and the presentation of the information is now being improved.

- **Predicting The Future:** In this phase the IT department starts to be able to help the rest of the company to predict and anticipate changes in their operating conditions. This is accomplished through the use of statistical models and algorithms that are tuned to the data available and the environment in which the business operates.

- **Usage:** In this phase, the knowledge coming out of the IT department is no longer just contained in a report. Instead, the information is being put to use when it becomes available. The information is starting to be used as a part of the company's day-to-day operations.

- **Transformation:** In the final phase, the analytical results from processing the data change the company from where it was into a more efficient company that relies on its IT department to show it how to better compete in its market and become more successful.

What All of This Means for You

Just having a lot of data does a CIO no good. You need to understand how you are going to **apply analytics to that data** in order to extract the information that your business is going to need you to get for them.

Every IT department goes through a set of 7 phases as they come to grips with how they are going to deal with the arrival of Big Data. They progress from simply struggling to deal with the quantity of data that they are faced with to finding ways to **use the data to transform the business**.

People in the CIO position find themselves in a very interesting position: they are sitting on top of an incredibly valuable resource: all of the data that the company collects. Now they need to find ways to take action and by using analytics turn that data into **knowledge that the company can use**. By following the 7 step process that we've discussed, CIOs can conquer the Big Data beast and give the rest of the company what they are looking for from the IT department.

Chapter 5

CIOs Need to Be on the Lookout for Proprietary Solutions Disguised as Standards

Chapter 5: CIOs Need To Be On the Lookout for Proprietary Solutions Disguised As Standards

As the person with the CIO job, you are always on the lookout for ways to simplify what the IT department is doing in order to boost the importance of information technology within your company.

One way to make this happen is to have the department **adopt the use of standards**. You would think that that would be the end of it; however, those vendors are sneaky devils and you need to be careful that you don't select a standard that is really a proprietary solution in disguise.

Why Adopt Standards?

Isn't the whole idea of IT to be free? To do **that innovation thing** and to not be restricted by artificial constraints on what tools and methods are available to your department? The answer is, of course, yes and no.

It turns out that standards are a good thing. A standard is where an IT department agrees to use the same set of terminology to reduce the possibility that people in the IT department are going to get confused. If we can all agree on which standard to use, then we can **reduce both the time and the resources** that a given task is going to require.

What we all need to keep in mind is that we can't choose to use a standard just because it exists. Rather, we always need to be looking for **the business reason** for the standard to exist. Once we've been able to identify this, then we will be able to understand why we are willing to put up with the restriction of our options that the use of the standard causes.

What Are Proprietary "Standards"?

If I've been able to convince you that standards are a good thing, then we have only one more thing to discuss: **bad standards**. The future of IT lies in such technologies as "the cloud" and this is causing a problem for IT vendors. What used to be clearly differentiated hardware and software products are very quickly becoming commoditized offerings where everything looks the same.

As you might expect, **vendors are scrambling to make their products look different from everyone else's**. One way that they are doing this is by offering what are called "blended systems" that offer you the promise of implementing a standards based solution; however, they are really tricking you into implementing their proprietary solution.

What vendors are doing is combining elements that may be standardized, such as servers, with tightly integrated proprietary elements. Anytime you see a vendor describing some aspect of their solution as being **"unique"** you should be very, very careful. This all may look great on paper; however, once you have it implemented, you are going to see costs of hardware maintenance start to skyrocket on you.

What Does All Of This Mean For You?

The job of any IT department is to provide the best solutions at the lowest cost to the rest of the company. Given the complexity of a modern IT solution, this can be a challenge to do. When you are in the CIO position, you have the ability to select IT standards that you want to implement in your department and this can simplify life for everyone. However, make sure that **you don't select any vendor proprietary solutions** that are disguised as a standard.

A standard is a limiting set of rules that simplify life for the IT department that implements it. Yes, you are giving up some decision making; however, you are also **simplifying life for your staff**. Vendors will try to sneak in their proprietary solutions in order to get you to adopt them and then be locked in to their products. Keep your eyes open and don't let this happen to you.

Chapter 6

CIOs Need to Plan for the End of a Cloud Relationship

Chapter 6: CIOs Need To Plan For the End of a Cloud Relationship

Since the cloud is a new and shiny thing in the world of IT departments, we are all excited about it because it now has a lot to do with the importance of information technology. Part of having the CIO job is spending your day thinking about **how you can move more of the company's applications into the cloud**. However, it turns out that there is an aspect of this cloud stuff that CIOs have not been spending enough time thinking about: what to do when the relationship is over…

Problems with Breaking Up With Your Cloud Vendor

I'm pretty sure that we can all understand the excitement that CIOs feel as they prepare to move yet another company application into the cloud. The promise of reduced operating costs, fewer IT staff, and **virtually unlimited growth** all combine to make this seem like a no-brainer. However, what more and more CIOs are now discovering is that your relationship with your cloud vendor won't last forever.

When you decide to bring a cloud based application back in house or switch it over to another cloud vendor, **this is when problems can start to show up**. The questions of just exactly who owns your data and what tools you are going to use to extract your data from the cloud need to be answered. These answers just might surprise you.

This all comes down to having a CIO do his or her due diligence before getting into bed with a cloud vendor. From the beginning CIOs need to be considering what it is going to take **in order to be able to switch cloud vendors**. If they don't, then they just may discover that breaking up with their cloud vendor is more expensive, complicated, and painful than they expected.

Things to Consider Up Front

If we can all acknowledge that breaking up with your current cloud vendor can be a difficult thing to do, **what steps should a CIO be taking right now?** It all comes down to realizing that you may have a problem from the start. You are going to have to make sure that the breakup is covered in your contract with your cloud vendor.

Two of the key issues that you need to resolve with your cloud vendor right off the bat are **who owns your data** and how can you gain access to it. Another important question that many CIOs don't think to work out is how many copies of your data that you would want to receive if you decided to move your data to another cloud vendor.

Your ultimate solution to this challenge **needs to be done in multiple layers**. What this means is that, of course, your contract with your cloud vendor needs to specify that you own your data and that you need to receive copies of it should the relationship end. However, you then need to go deeper. The contract needs to spell out how you physically get your data back, who pays for it, is it encrypted, and the form of the data and the file type that you'll be receiving it in.

What All of This Means for You

If you are in the CIO position, then you have undoubtedly gotten caught up in the "cloud madness" that is currently sweeping through the IT industry. We are all well aware of the benefits of moving our IT applications to the cloud. However, it turns out that we also need to spend time **thinking about how we would go about switching cloud vendors**.

When you switch cloud vendors, you are faced with the challenge of getting your company's data out of their cloud so that you can move it to a new cloud. If you haven't planned for this, then **it could turn out to be expensive**. When you're setting up your cloud contract, make sure you specify how you'll get your data, how many copies of your data you'll get, and what format you'll get it in.

The good news is that cloud vendors need you just as much as you need them. It's not in their own best interest to part ways with you on bad terms. However, they are in business to make money and **they'll try to charge you to leave them**. Work out the details when you two are still dating and when it comes time to break up the marriage, everything will go a lot smoother.

Chapter 7

Big Data Means 5 Big Problems for CIOs

Chapter 7: Big Data Means 5 Big Problems for CIOs

If you pick up just about any IT magazine these days, you'll see that everyone seems to have decided that we are now living in the age of "big data". No data set is too large to be processed by your IT department. The rest of the company now understands the importance of information technology and they believe that all you have to do is drop the data in and **magically actionable information** should pop out that the entire company can start to use today.

Well, as with all things in life, it's never quite that easy. Those of us who have the CIO job are starting to learn that along with big data **comes some very large problems** that we are going to have to find a way to solve. Let's spend a moment and talk about 5 of these "big" problems...

5 Big Data Problems That CIOs Need To Solve

The one thing that no CIO wants to have happen is for his or her IT department to get involved in a big data project **that ends up delivering nothing**. The reason that this can happen to a big data project is that a company makes a mistake and the end result is that the project gets scrapped. Here are 5 common big data project mistakes and how to avoid making them:

- <u>Garbage In....</u>: Just having a lot of data is not enough to have a successful big data project. The company has to have a very clear idea of what questions they are trying to have answered before the big data project gets started. The mistake that too many companies make is that they believe that just by processing the data, answers will magically show up. It doesn't work this way – you have to know what you are looking for before the project starts.

- **Not Enough of The Right People:** It turns out that performing complex analysis of big data sets is actually hard work. It takes a special kind of person with a unique set of skills. Right now there are not a lot of these people out there. If your IT department does not have the right people, then you'll never be successful. Now is the time to identify the people who have the right skill sets. Have them get additional training and make sure that they are ready when your next big data project starts.

- **Organization Counts:** Just exactly where is all of the data that you are going to want to process? All too often companies have things like customer data spread across multiple databases. This means that the big data project is going to have to spend time looking for different pieces of data in different locations even before the main analysis starts. Take the time to pull together all of the data that you are going to need into a single database so that you can focus your department's time and energy on what really counts.

- **Fight!:** Everyone in the company knows the importance of big data and everyone wants to be the first to get their hands on the results of the project. If as CIO you allow this to happen, internal departments are going to be spending their time fighting with each other. As the senior IT person, you need to set the tone from the top – the data belongs to the company and the results belong to the company, no department has preference over any other department.

- **Setting The Bar Too High:** It can be too easy to create a big data project that has really big goals. When you do this, the possibility of the project failing or ending up under delivering is boosted. Don't make this mistake. Instead, start out by setting a smaller objective and keep your goals narrow. What will happen is that this smaller project will be a success. You can then build on it and go on to create larger projects that will have a much better chance of being successful.

What All of This Means for You

We have entered an age where all of a sudden CIOs are discovering that their IT departments are **no long limited by the amount of computing power that their budget can purchase**. With the arrival of cloud computing, an almost unlimited amount of processing power is now available to process the enormous amount of data that every company is collecting.

What this means is that in order to be able to deliver to the company what they are expecting to get out of their big data, if you are sitting in the CIO position then you are going to have to first **solve some big data related problems**. These include making sure that they have the right data to process, finding the right IT staff to do the work, organizing the data, resolving differences between data owners, and making sure that the IT department does not over promise.

Yes, great things can come from finally having the computing horsepower needed to process enormous amounts of data. However, before you can deliver to the company the useful results that they are looking for, you are first going to have to **solve the big problems that come along with your big data**.

Chapter 8

Questions about the Cloud that Every CIO Should Be Asking

Chapter 8: Questions about the Cloud That Every CIO Should Be Asking

I like clouds, you like clouds, everyone likes clouds. CIOs everywhere are getting inundated with cloud requests, cloud proposals, and cloud projects. However, **committing your company's IT assets to the cloud is a big deal** considering the importance of information technology to the company. This sure seems like the kind of thing that you don't want to just rush into. What kind of important questions should a CIO be asking now before you make the commitment to the cloud?

6 Important Cloud Questions That CIOs Need to Answer

When faced with having to make decisions about just how involved in cloud computing your company should be, a CIO is facing a great number of unknowns. The whole area of clouds is brand new and so there is not always a lot of good information for you to use. That's why **asking the right questions about clouds** is so very important. Here are 6 questions that every CIO should be asking before they jump into the cloud:

- **TCO?:** The Total Cost of Ownership (TCO) of cloud computing is not free, no matter what some of the articles that you've read have told you. However, as the person with the CIO job you are going to have to ask some questions about if it is cheaper to run your applications in the cloud or on servers owned by the company. Very few IT departments can accurately tell how much it costs to run a specific application (depreciated capex, opex, all associated labor). There is a very good chance that the cloud will be cheaper, but you need to ask the questions in order to find out.

- **Who Manages the Cloud?:** When it comes to managing the vendor who provides the cloud, it's not always in your best interest as CIO to have the IT department perform this task. This is more of a question of understanding how to do financial management on a per application basis. Your IT department is going to have to work with the finance department in order to get the answers that you are going to need.

- **Just How Safe Is Your Company's Data?:** Any time your company's data leaves the building, you have just changed your risk profile. You need to make sure that you can trust the vendor who is providing you with cloud services. However, studies have shown that most cloud vendors do a better job of protecting the data in their data centers than most companies do. You are probably in good hands; however, take the time to confirm this.

- **Outage?:** No cloud provider is perfect – they all experience outages at some point in time. You need to expect this to occur. The big question is just how much risk is the company facing and how would you handle it. Many CIOs end up splitting their cloud deployment between multiple vendors just because of this issue.

- **What If the Cloud Vendor Goes Away?:** Any business can fail and your cloud vendor is no different than anyone else. What this means for you is that you always have to have a backup plan – where would you go if your vendor went away. Minimize the chances of this happening to you by taking the time before you sign a contract to fully check out your vendor and make sure that they carry insurance.

- **How to Start?:** Entering into the world of cloud computing can be a big step for any company. In order to get started, first you are going to need to do a complete inventory of all of the applications that the company is currently using. Next, you are going to have to find a cloud provider who specializes in supporting your type of business. Finally, you are going to need to create a set of service-level expectations so that you have a good understanding of what you want to get from your cloud provider.

What All of This Means for You

CIOs have to be very careful when it comes to making decisions about what to do about cloud computing. Cloud is a hot buzz word right now and it could be easy to commit too much to the cloud too early. What the person in the CIO position need to do is to **take the time to ask the right questions about clouds** and make sure that they get the answers that they need before they proceed.

The questions that need to be answered include **what the total cost of ownership is**, who is going to manage the cloud, the overall safety of corporate data in the cloud and what happens to the data if there is a cloud outage, the financial stability of the cloud provider, and what the best way to get started with a cloud is.

CIOs that read the IT trade journals might get the mistaken impression that they are behind the times when it comes to clouds. The reality is that **it's still early on in the life of this new IT technology**. Don't make the mistake and rush in. Instead, take your time and proceed cautiously. Ask the right questions, get the right answers and then you'll know what you have to do.

Chapter 9

Why CIOs Need to Get Good at Reusing Technology

Chapter 9: Why CIOs Need To Get Good At Reusing Technology

I'm sure that you know that you shouldn't throw things that can be recycled away. Save the planet and all of that. So this brings up an interesting question: as a CIO **how committed to recycling technology are you** when the company is preparing to start up a brand new project?

Why It Makes Sense to Recycle Technology

When your company is starting up a new project, there can be a great deal of excitement in the air. Everything about the project is new, and so it can be very easy to decide that the technology that the project will be using should be new also. The thinking is that "we're different" and therefore **the technology that we use should be different also**. However, this may be the wrong decision.

The problem with this thinking is that **it turns out that it may cause more problems than it solves**. Specifically, studies done by MIT's Sloan Center for Information Systems Research has revealed that by reusing existing technology the risk of a new project can be lowered. Specifically, firms that are able to share existing technology across departments and business units discover that they are able to grow faster and are able to keep their costs lower than firms that don't do this.

If you are able to reuse your technology on a new project, this is going to free your time up. You won't be distracted by all of the issues that come along with rolling a new technology out to a highly visible project. Instead, the use of the existing technology will allow the person with the CIO job to focus on innovation and **deliver what the company expects you to provide – results**.

How to Go About Recycling Technology

Recycling technology is something that can't be left up to the part of the IT department that will be assigned to work on the new project. They will be justifiably excited about the new project and may not have the ability to see the recycling opportunities. Instead, the person in the CIO position needs to **establish an IT team that will be responsible for recycling the company's IT resources** and can lend a hand when a new project is starting up.

One of the biggest reasons that technology recycling may not be adopted by your company may be because of who's in charge. Management needs to buy in to the idea of reusing existing IT resources. In order to make this happen the CIO needs to **establish processes** that will cause reuse to occur. Making reuse part of any project proposal can play a key role in making sure that reuse is included from the start of the project planning cycle.

In order for any technology reuse program to be successful, **the culture of the company is going to have to change**. This means that the CIO is going to have to make sure that the rest of the company knows about the successes that come about because of IT recycling efforts. Getting the word out is the first step in making this happen and it's something that has to be done every day.

What All of This Means for You

When CIOs are faced with starting up a new project, it can be very tempting to go out and get all new hardware and software to support the shiny new project. However, the savvy CIO realizes that if they can find a way to **reuse the technology that they already have**, they'll boost the project's chances of success.

Using well established technology **reduces the risk that comes with using any IT technology as a part of a critical project**. It is the role of the CIO to make it easier for the company to reuse existing IT resources. Part of doing this is to clearly establish who gets to make these kinds of decisions. This may require an effort to change the culture of the company.

The benefits of reusing existing IT technology will become obvious very quickly. As project risk goes down and IT is seen as an enabler and not a hindrance, **the importance of information technology, and of course the CIO, to the company will increase**.

Chapter 10

When It Comes to Data Mining – Is the CIO in Charge?

Chapter 10: When It Comes To Data Mining – Is The CIO In Charge?

With all of this talk about cloud computing, it can be easy to forget about yesterday's hot topic: **data mining**. However, it turns out that cloud computing just makes doing data mining a whole lot easier. This means that data mining is reminding the company about the importance of information technology and is staging a comeback. The person with the CIO job is going to have to start to allocate time to deal with this. How about if we take a look at where things currently stand?

Why Bother Doing Data Mining?

As with most things in business, **the motivation for spending the time to do data mining comes down to money**. There are two different reasons that companies give for mining their data. According to the IBM Institute for Business Value 2013 Big Data & Analytics Study, 70% of firms who were doing data mining were doing it in order to boost their revenues. The other 30% stated that they were doing it in order to cut costs.

Data mining does not come free or cheap. It takes time, energy, and a great deal of human labor to collect and process all of that data. In the report, 60% of the companies that were doing data mining reported that **they saw a return on their investment in data mining within the first year**. However, all was not perfect even at these firms.

What appears to be lacking is **any sort of guidance or leadership from the top of the company**. This lack of top-down guidance prevents the different departments that are involved from fully trusting each other. This coupled with a lack of staff with the required unique skills that data mining requires can cause a company's data mining efforts to stall.

Who's In Charge Of A Company's Data Mining Work?

Any data mining effort can be a large undertaking for a company. In order for it to work out, **a strong leader needs to be in charge of the company's big data efforts**. A significant problem is that exactly who that person is seems to differ from company to company.

The CIO has been identified as leading the company's data mining efforts **at only 15% of the companies surveyed**, 14% of the efforts were being led by the CEO and 8% were being led by the CFO. This may explain why so many companies are having difficulties getting their various departments to work together.

Every company has to make their own decision about **who within the firm will be working on the data mining project**. At 14% of the firms, data mining experts were shared between departments. At 22% of the firms the IT department was solely responsible for all things related to data mining. In 30% of the firms each separate business unit was responsible for doing its own data mining. Finally, at 34% of the firms, a separate specialized analytics unit had been created to only do data mining.

What Does All Of This Mean For You?

In order for a company to determine how it should best spend its time, it needs to take a look at what its current customers are trying to tell it. The best way to go about doing this is to mine the enormous amount of customer, product, and market data that every company collects.

Data mining is a complex and complicated task. Companies are motivated to do data mining because **they believe that it will have a positive impact on their revenues**. The person in the CIO position has to be deeply involved in this process. Since it turns out that only 15% of CIOs are leading the big data charge, clearly many CIOs still need to wake up to their new responsibility.

Data mining is clearly an IT task that will have an impact for the entire company. **CIOs are the executive who is best suited to understand what the company wants to accomplish and to know how to make it happen**. Take the time to talk with the rest of the company's executive team and then get busy – your data is waiting to be mined!

Chapter 11

The Problem with Glitches

Chapter 11: The Problem with Glitches

In a perfect world, IT systems would always work and they would always work correctly. However, we don't live in that perfect world. What this **means for CIOs is that glitches happen**. It's our job to minimize them, but we'll never be able to eliminate them completely. We're always going to have to come up with a plan for dealing with them and their aftermath when they do occur. U.S. Stock Exchanges, who know about the importance of information technology, had their fair share of glitches in 2013. I wonder how their CIOs are planning dealing with the aftermath of that?

The Role of the Securities and Exchange Commission

In the United States, trading of stocks and bonds is overseen by the Securities and Exchange Commission (SEC). In 2013, a series of glitches in the stock markets were severe enough to **gain the attention of the SEC**. On May 6, 2010, there was the so-called "flash crash" in which the stock markets plunged in a very short period of time. This alerted the world to the fact that glitches could affect modern stock markets. On August 22, 2013, a breakdown of a data feed from the NASDAQ halted trading in more than 2,700 stocks for over three hours.

Clearly these glitches were occurring within the IT departments of the stock market IT systems. **It was up to the person with the CIO job to fix them**. The attention of the SEC meant that now the world was watching and it was up to the CIO to create a solution.

In the short term, the SEC has now proposed **a new set of rules** for the stock market CIOs and their IT departments to implement. These rules have to do with the maintenance and testing of the trading systems that run the stock market. There has been some initial resistance to the new rules by CIOs because they will be expensive to implement.

Possible Glitch Fixes

If glitches like the August 22, 2013 outage can't be completely prevented, then what is to be done? CIO's need to create plans for **how to deal with a glitch when it is happening** and then what to do in the aftermath of the glitch.

Stock market CIOs are now looking into ways that they can **improve the computer-driven data feeds** that are used to report the trades that have been executed on the stock exchanges. Additionally, the various players in the stock market need to start to do a better job of coordinating their testing on changes to their systems before they are rolled out into production in order to prevent the occurrence of unplanned outages.

There has been additional talk about implementing so called **"kill-switches"** that would allow the stock markets to be shut down if something bad starts to occur. This all leads to the fact that the various parties also need to create a way to coordinate their actions for restarting the stock markets after a glitch induced shut down has occurred.

What All of This Means for You

Glitches happen. Even the best CIOs can't stop them. However, what we all can do is to **come up with ways to deal with them when they do happen** and then manage the aftermath.

The problems with the U.S. Stock Exchanges in 2013 clearly proved the **glitches can happen to even the best funded IT departments**. In this case, the impact of the glitches was so great that that federal government in the form of the Securities and Exchange Commission (SEC) had to step in. Plans for dealing with future glitches include having the person in the CIO position create coordination between firms on testing and creating plans for how markets could be reopened after a shut down.

We can't stop future glitches from happening – that's just the way that life is. Instead, we need to take steps to deal with glitches when they do occur. Additionally, taking the time today to **create plans for how the impact of the glitch can be dealt with** will solve tomorrow's problems before they happen.

Chapter 12

Perhaps the IT Help Desk Is No Longer Needed?

Chapter 12: Perhaps The IT Help Desk Is No Longer Needed?

Just in case you've been living under a rock for the past few years, one of the biggest crazes to sweep through the world of IT has been **the BYOD trend: "Bring Your Own Device" (to work)**.

The thinking is that workers have been purchasing and using such sophisticated electronic devices in their personal lives and because of the importance of information technology it no longer really made sense for their company to provide them with lesser quality devices.

Instead, workers should bring in their own personal phone, tablet, etc. and use them at work. What we all thought would happen, never did...

Where's The Spike?

People who have the CIO job were dreading the arrival of the BYOD craze. The thinking was that IT help desks were going to be **flooded with requests** from end users for help with a virtually unlimited number of personal communications devices. However, the exact opposite has happened – help desk call volume has gone down.

There were two reasons that this occurred. The first is that the Internet contains a vast collection of information on **how end users can solve their own problems with their devices**. It is often easier to do a search with Google than to call the company's help desk. Additionally, the mobile device management software that firms have started to use has reached a level of functionality that many problems with mobile devices can now be fixed remotely.

The arrival of the Millennial worker in the modern workplace means that **there are now more tech-savvy workers**. They are less prone to pick up the phone and call the help desk and more likely to either talk with friends about their problems or do their own online research. Some firms have tried to help by creating shared online communities of workers that allow workers with the same types of devices to exchange suggestions and tips for getting their devices to work with the company's various systems.

What Does This Mean for the IT Help Desk Long Term?

Clearly, there are changes happening in the rest of the company that are going to **affect both the role of the IT help desk and the CIO**. Gartner, the IT industry analyst group, is forecasting a 25% – 30% drop in IT help desk call volume by 2016. The value that the IT help desk brings to the company is clearly decreasing.

This change is opening the door for CIOs to make dramatic changes to **how the IT department provides support to the rest of the company**. More and more firms are creating peer-to-peer support networks where employees help each other with IT related problems. In order for these networks to work, the IT department needs to have installed the tools that will allow the various people to connect with each other and to exchange information.

Taking things one step further, some CIOs are creating so called "genius bars" at work. Modeled after the technology experts that can be found at Apple retail stores, these knowledgeable subject matter experts are able to **quickly and easily resolve even the most difficult end user IT issues.**

What Does All Of This Mean For You?

The world is changing and IT is going to have to change with it. The arrival of BYOD in the modern workplace is going to have **a lasting impact on the world of IT**. Specifically, it's going to change how the traditional IT help desk operates.

When the BYOD craze started, it was anticipated that there would be **a spike in calls to the company help desk**. However, the exact opposite has occurred: call volumes have gone down. In fact, call volumes are forecasted to continue to decrease over the next few years. What this means for IT is that the traditional help desk function has to be reshaped. Providing fewer people who have deeper levels of understanding of the company's IT operations is what will be required going forward.

The person in the CIO position is going to have to learn how to deal with the changes that are happening in the rest of the company. What used to work in terms of IT help desks will not work in the future. You are going to need to educate the rest of the company about **the help desk changes that will be happening** and make sure that everyone's needs are taken care of. Welcome to a brave new era of help desk support!

It's from the forge of failure that the steel of success is formed.

Hard Work Does Not Guarantee Success, But Success Does Not Happen Without Hard Work.

- Dr. Jim Anderson

Create IT Departments That Are Productive And A Valuable Asset To The Rest Of The Company!

Dr. Jim Anderson is available to provide training and coaching on the topics that are the most important to people who have to manage IT departments: how can I build a productive IT department (and keep it together) while at the same time providing the rest of the company with the IT services that they need?

Dr. Anderson believes that in order to both learn and remember what he says, speakers need to laugh. Each one of his speeches is full of fun and humor so that what he says "sticks" with everyone.

Dr. Anderson's CIO SkillsTraining Includes:

4. How to identify and attract the right type of IT workers to your IT department.
5. How to build relationships with the company's senior management in order to get the support that you need?
6. How to stay on top of changing technology and security issues so that you never get surprised?

Dr. Jim Anderson works with over 100 customers per year. To invite Dr. Anderson to work with you, contact him at:

Phone: 813-418-6970 or
Email: jim@BlueElephantConsulting.com

Photo Credits:

Cover - By: Pacific Northwest National Laboratory
https://www.flickr.com/photos/pnnl/

Chapter 1 - By: macwagen
https://www.flickr.com/photos/macwagen/

Chapter 2 - By: Daniel Rehn
https://www.flickr.com/photos/daniel-rehn/

Chapter 3 - By: U.S. Department of Agriculture
https://www.flickr.com/photos/usdagov/

Chapter 4 - By: Duncan Rawlinson
https://www.flickr.com/photos/thelastminute/

Chapter 5 - By: Esther Simpson
https://www.flickr.com/photos/estherase/

Chapter 6 - By: Theophilos Papadopouls
https://www.flickr.com/photos/theo_reth/

Chapter 7 - By: infocux Technologies
https://www.flickr.com/photos/infocux/

Chapter 8 - By: theaucitron
https://www.flickr.com/photos/theaucitron/

Chapter 9 - By: Chin
https://www.flickr.com/photos/eleven/

Chapter 10 - By: State Library of South Australia
https://www.flickr.com/photos/state_library_south_australia/

Chapter 11 - By: bfishadow
https://www.flickr.com/photos/bfishadow/

Chapter 12 - By: stans_pat_pix
https://www.flickr.com/photos/34219731@N07/

Other Books By The Author

Product Management

- How Product Managers Can Grow Their Career: How Product Managers Can Find And Succeed In The Right Job

- Product Management Secrets: Techniques For Product Managers To Boost Product Sales And Increase Customer Satisfaction

- Product Development Lessons For Product Managers: How Product Managers Can Create Successful Products

- Customer Lessons For Product Managers: Techniques For Product Managers To Better Understand What Their Customers Really Want

- Product Failure Lessons For Product Managers: Examples Of Products That Have Failed For Product Managers To Learn From

- Communication Skills For Product Managers: The Communication Skills That Product Managers Need To Know How To Use In Order To Have A Successful

Product

- How To Have A Successful Product Manager Career: The Things That You Need To Be Doing TODAY In Order To Have A Successful Product Manager Career

- Product Manager Product Success: How to keep your product on track and make it become a success

Public Speaking

- Plan For Success: How To Plan Your Next Speech: How to plan a speech in order to achieve your goals and delight your audience

- How To Become A Better Speaker By Changing How You Speak: Change techniques that will transform a speech into a memorable event

- How To Give A Great Presentation: Presentation techniques that will transform a speech into a memorable event

- How To Rehearse In Order To Give The Perfect Speech: How to effectively rehearse your next speech to that your message be remembered forever!

- Secrets To Creating The Perfect Speech: How to create a speech that will make your message be remembered forever!

- Secrets To Organizing The Perfect Speech: How to organize the best speech of your life!

- Secrets To Planning The Perfect Speech: How to plan to give the best speech of your life

- How To Show What You Mean During A Presentation: How to use visual techniques to transform a speech into a memorable event

CIO Skills

- What CIOs Need To Know About Working With Partners: Techniques For CIOs To Use In Order To Be Able To Successfully Work With Partners

- Critical CIO Management Skills: Decision Making Skills That Every CIO Needs To Have In Order To Be Able To Make The Right Choices

- How CIOs Can Make Innovation Happen: Tips And Techniques For CIOs To Use In Order To Make Innovation Happen In Their IT Department

- CIO Communication Skills Secrets: Tips And Techniques For CIOs To Use In Order To Become Better Communicators

- Managing Your CIO Career: Steps That CIOs Have To Take In Order To Have A Long And Successful Career

- CIO Business Skills: How CIOs can work effectively with the rest of the company!

IT Manager Skills

- How IT Managers Can Make Innovation Happen: Tips And Techniques For IT Managers To Use In Order To Make Innovation Happen In Their Teams

- Staffing Skills IT Managers Must Have: Tips And Techniques That IT Managers Can Use In Order To Correctly Staff Their Teams

- Secrets Of Effective Leadership For IT Managers: Tips And Techniques That IT Managers Can Use In Order To Develop Leadership Skills

- IT Manager Career Secrets: Tips And Techniques That IT Managers Can Use In Order To Have A Successful Career

- IT Manager Budgeting Skills: How IT Managers Can Request, Manage, Use, And Track Their Funding

<u>Negotiating</u>

- Learn How To Signal In Your Next Negotiation: How To Develop The Skill Of Effective Signaling In A Negotiation In Order To Get The Best Possible Outcome

- Learn The Skill Of Exploring In A Negotiation: How To Develop The Skill Of Exploring What Is Possible In A Negotiation In Order To Reach The Best Possible Deal

- Learn How To Argue In Your Next Negotiation: How To Develop The Skill Of Effective Arguing In A Negotiation In Order To Get The Best Possible Outcome

- How To Open Your Next Negotiation: How To Start A Negotiation In Order To Get The Best Possible Outcome

- Preparing For Your Next Negotiation: What You Need To Do BEFORE A Negotiation Starts In Order To Get The Best Possible Deal

Miscellaneous

- The Internet-Enabled Successful School District Superintendent: How To Use The Internet To Boost Parental Involvement In Your Schools

- Power Distribution Unit (PDU) Secrets: What Everyone Who Works In A Data Center Needs To Know!

- Making The Jump: How To Land Your Dream Job When You Get Out Of College!

How CIOs Can Stay On Top Of The Changes In The Technology That Powers The Company

> This book has been written with one goal in mind – to show you how you can stay on top of all of the changes that are occurring in the technologies that your company uses. Master these technologies today and your company will thank you!
>
> ## Let's Make Your CIO Career A Success!

What You'll Find Inside:

- **THE 7 STAGES OF BIG DATA ANALYTICS THAT EVERY CIO NEEDS TO KNOW ABOUT**
- **CIOS NEED TO PLAN FOR THE END OF A CLOUD RELATIONSHIP**
- **WHY CIOS NEED TO GET GOOD AT REUSING TECHNOLOGY**
- **WHEN IT COMES TO DATA MINING – IS THE CIO IN CHARGE?**

Dr. Jim Anderson brings his 25 years of real-world experience to this book. He's been a senior IT executive at some of the world's largest firms. He's going to show you what you need to do (and not do!) in order to make your CIO career a success!

www.ingramcontent.com/pod-product-compliance
Lightning Source LLC
Chambersburg PA
CBHW071800170526
45167CB00003B/1104